A BUSINESS APPROACH TO PUMPKIN FARMING

I0429998

Complete Entrepreneurial Step By Step Guide To Pumpkin Garden From Scratch

ZHURI HART

DISCLAIMER

This book is intended to provide general information and insights on adopting a business approach to farming. The content within is based on the author's knowledge and experiences up to the date of publication. It is essential to recognize that the field of agriculture is dynamic, influenced by various factors such as market conditions, climate, and regulatory changes.

Readers are advised to conduct thorough research, seek professional advice, and consider their unique circumstances before implementing any strategies or practices discussed in this book. The author and publisher disclaim any responsibility for the accuracy, completeness, or suitability of the information provided. The book is not a substitute for professional advice, and the author and publisher shall not be liable for any damages or losses arising from the use or reliance on the information presented herein.

Individual results may vary, and success in farming enterprises is contingent upon numerous variables. The author encourages readers to consult with relevant experts, agricultural extension services, and legal or financial professionals to tailor strategies to their specific needs and local conditions.

This book is not intended to be a comprehensive guide to all aspects of farming, and readers should exercise their judgment and discretion in applying the principles discussed. The author and publisher do not endorse any specific products, services, or companies mentioned in this book unless explicitly stated.

By reading this book, the reader acknowledges and accepts the inherent uncertainties in agricultural endeavors and agrees to use the information at their own risk.

TABLE OF CONTENTS

ABOUT THE BOOK

"A Business Approach to Pumpkin Farming," a book, provides a thorough overview for those looking to start or expand their pumpkin farming business. The book gives background information and an overview in the Introduction, explaining why pumpkin cultivation is important and profitable. It explores this agriculture sector's business potential and highlights its importance in the present market environment. The book's stated goals are in line with giving readers the information and abilities needed for profitable pumpkin farming business ventures.

A comprehensive analysis of the pumpkin industry is started, which provides a historical overview, market information, and a look at new trends and prospects. This basic knowledge lays the groundwork, which walks readers through the vital first stages of establishing a pumpkin farm. This section covers several important subjects, including planning farm layouts, choosing suitable pumpkin types, and assessing preparedness.

Crop management and soil preparation are covered in detail. Soil testing, additives, and efficient irrigation techniques are highlighted. The next chapters offer helpful advice on post-harvest handling, harvesting methods, and planting and growing pumpkins. The book provides readers with the fundamental information required to guarantee a profitable and long-lasting pumpkin-growing business.

The book delves deeper than only cultivation to discuss business-related topics. The book's practical utility is enhanced by essential elements such as marketing and selling tactics, detailed guidance on business management, financial planning, and risk reduction. In addition, it delves into the necessity of sustainability and ecological factors in pumpkin cultivation, mirroring the current emphasis on conscientious farming methods.

The book offers helpful ideas for problem-solving and adaptation, as well as an anticipation of common issues faced by pumpkin farmers. The book intends to provide readers with the tools they need to negotiate obstacles in their pursuit of pumpkin growing by addressing probable difficulties. All things considered, "A Business Approach to Pumpkin Farming" is a valuable book that combines agricultural knowledge with commercial savvy to promote success in the exciting and dynamic field of pumpkin farming.

CHAPTER ONE

PUMPKIN FARMING INTRODUCTION

CONTEXT AND SYNOPSIS

Pumpkin farming is one of the most diverse and profitable agricultural endeavors that has seen tremendous growth in the last few years. From their humble beginnings as seasonal decorations, pumpkins have developed to be an essential part of many different culinary customs, from soups and pies to a variety of celebratory dishes. Pumpkins are native to North America. This farming method has spread across international borders and become a common sight in many agricultural landscapes.

WHY GROW PUMPKINS?

Several characteristics that make pumpkin growing appealing to both farmers and businesspeople serve as the foundation for the choice to get started. First of all, pumpkins are a robust crop to cultivate since they are hardy and show a high level of resistance to pests and illnesses. Their capacity to adapt to many climatic conditions adds to their appeal and allows farmers to include pumpkin growing in a range of agricultural environments.

Furthermore, the nutritional makeup of pumpkins confers still another level of importance on their production. Packed with vital vitamins, minerals, and antioxidants, pumpkins are a great addition to any diet and are becoming more and more known for their possible health advantages. Growing consumer knowledge of nutrition has led to an increase in demand for pumpkins and pumpkin-related items, which has made pumpkin farming a profitable business that can adapt to the changing needs of a health-conscious market.

THE FARMING OF PUMPKINS HAS BUSINESS POTENTIAL

Pumpkin cultivation has developed into a profitable industry with numerous revenue streams, surpassing its historical status as a seasonal crop. Because of their adaptability, pumpkins can be used to make a wide range of commercial commodities, from processed goods like canned pumpkin, pumpkin puree, and products based on pumpkin spices, to fresh produce for local markets.

The variety of products available increases the commercial potential of pumpkin growing by giving growers the chance to serve both domestic and international markets.

In addition, the growth of agro tourism has given pumpkin-growing business owners new opportunities. Pumpkin patches, harvest celebrations, and farm-to-table excursions have grown in popularity as tourist destinations, luring visitors looking for both a hands-on agricultural experience and fresh vegetables. This feature promotes community involvement and awareness of sustainable agricultural methods in addition to supporting the economic viability of pumpkin growing.

The agricultural industry of pumpkin cultivation is characterized by its versatility, nutritional value, and many commercial opportunities, making it a dynamic and resilient sector. In the ever-evolving world of agriculture and agribusiness, growing pumpkins offer a potential prospect for individuals looking for a profitable and sustainable business endeavor as customer preferences continue to change.

CHAPTER TWO

COMPREHENDING THE PUMPKIN SECTOR

A HISTORICAL VIEW OF PUMPKIN GROWING

Pumpkins were farmed for their nutritional worth and adaptability in ancient civilizations, which is where the historical perspective of pumpkin farming began. Pumpkins are native to North America and have a long history of blending in with native civilizations. Eventually, early immigrants used pumpkins in their meals. Pumpkins began as a simple food crop and over time developed into a cultural symbol. They are now widely used in fall harvest celebrations and, most famously, in the Halloween tradition of carving jack-o'-lanterns.

PRESENT SITUATION OF THE PUMPKIN INDUSTRY

The expectations and interests of consumers have changed significantly in the modern pumpkin market.

Pumpkins have evolved into a flexible element that can be used in a wide range of culinary dishes and drinks. They are no longer only thought of as seasonal decorations and pies. Specialty pumpkin cultivars are in higher demand in the market, which has led to a more varied product landscape.

Furthermore, improvements in processing methods have increased the shelf life of items made from pumpkin, making them convenient and available all year round.

Growing interest in organic and sustainable agricultural methods is one trend influencing the pumpkin farming sector. Farmers are adopting environmentally friendly production techniques as a result of growing consumer demand for pumpkins grown without the use of artificial pesticides and fertilizers. This change is in line with broader consumer trends toward making healthier and more ecologically friendly decisions, which gives pumpkin growers the chance to set themselves apart from the competition and carve out niche niches.

OPPORTUNITIES AND TRENDS IN PUMPKIN FARMING

The emergence of items made from pumpkins outside of conventional uses is another noteworthy trend. The industry is growing because pumpkin-flavored snacks, drinks, and even skincare products are becoming more and more popular. Farmers now have more opportunities to investigate value-added goods thanks to this diversification, which promotes creativity and cooperation within the sector.

Pumpkin cultivation offers opportunities not only in traditional markets but also in export markets due to the growing worldwide demand. Pumpkin varieties that were formerly exclusive to a certain region are now making their way into global markets as customers throughout the world grow increasingly interested in unique and varied culinary options. To take advantage of these opportunities, distributors, and farmers can work together in strategic partnerships and collaborations that will benefit all parties.

Furthermore, technology is essential to contemporary pumpkin farming since it provides cutting-edge approaches to supply chain optimization, precision agriculture, and crop management. Farmers are better able to increase output, decrease resource waste, and adjust to market changes with the help of automation and data-driven insights. Pumpkin growers who embrace technology can position themselves for long-term success in a dynamic and fiercely competitive agricultural environment.

The historical trajectory of the pumpkin business demonstrates its cultural relevance and flexibility over millennia. Due to shifting customer preferences, the market is currently showing signs of a transition towards a variety of year-round uses. To satisfy the changing needs of the global market, pumpkin farmers are being encouraged to remain adaptable and creative by adopting sustainable techniques and investigating new product options. These exciting trends and potential for pumpkin farming are presented here.

CHAPTER THREE

HOW TO BEGIN GROWING PUMPKINS

EVALUATION OF YOUR PREPAREDNESS

Before you start pumpkin farming, you should evaluate your level of preparedness for this type of farming. Take into account elements like your dedication, availability of time, and enthusiasm for farming. During the growth season, producing pumpkins requires constant care and work, so consider if you have the commitment needed to grow them successfully. Evaluate your physical endurance as well, since growing pumpkins frequently requires manual labor for tasks like planting, weeding, and harvesting.

COMPETENCIES AND INFORMATION

Having the right information and abilities is essential to running a successful pumpkin farm. Learn about fundamental agricultural techniques like pest management, irrigation, and soil preparation.

A more abundant harvest will result from knowing the particular requirements of pumpkins, such as ideal growing circumstances and possible obstacles. To improve your skills, go to classes, ask seasoned farmers for advice, and keep up with the most recent developments in pumpkin cultivation.

INVESTMENT AND RESOURCES

One must devote a substantial amount of time and financial resources to pumpkin farming. Examine the land that can be used for farming and make sure that it satisfies the necessary conditions for pumpkin development. Take into account elements like solar exposure, drainage, and soil condition. Determine how much it will cost to buy irrigation systems, seeds, fertilizer, and any other equipment that will be required. A well-planned budget can assist you in allocating resources and planning them effectively, lowering the chance of overspending and guaranteeing a profitable farming operation.

CHOOSING THE BEST TYPES OF PUMPKINS

Selecting the right variety of pumpkins is essential to farming success. When choosing pumpkin breeds, take market demand, soil type, and climate into account. Certain types could be adapted to a given area or possess a special resistance to pests and illnesses. For information on which pumpkin varieties grow well in your particular environment, look up the most well-liked varieties in your area and speak with the local agricultural extension agencies. You can potentially boost your overall production and accommodate different market preferences by diversifying your pumpkin types.

ORGANIZING AND CREATING A PUMPKIN FARM

A well-planned layout and design are necessary for a pumpkin farm to run smoothly. Start by sketching the arrangement of your farm, considering elements like accessibility, row spacing, and spacing. Ample irrigation systems should be planned for, as pumpkins need constant moisture during the growing season. To preserve the health of the soil, think about incorporating crop rotation techniques and sustainable farming methods. Establish a schedule for planting, caring for, and harvesting that takes into account the environment and growth season in your area. To guarantee a seamless transfer from the farm to the market, don't forget to account for storage and transportation logistics.

A thorough assessment of your preparedness, the acquisition of critical abilities and information, prudent resource management, deliberate variety selection, and painstaking planning and design of your pumpkin farm are all necessary for successful pumpkin farming. By taking care of these fundamental ideas, you may build a strong basis for a profitable and long-lasting pumpkin farming endeavor.

CHAPTER FOUR

GETTING READY FOR SOIL AND MANAGING CROPS

SOIL TESTING AND ANALYSIS

Proper soil preparation and crop management depend heavily on soil testing and analysis. Understanding the composition, pH, and nutrient levels of the soil is crucial before starting any kind of agricultural venture. Soil testing is the process of taking soil samples from various fields and depths, which are then subjected to a variety of analytical procedures.

Farmers can make well-informed decisions on the selection and use of fertilizers thanks to this thorough analysis, which offers insightful information about the fertility status of the soil.

Farmers can customize their crop production methods based on the data gathered from soil testing. Growers can enhance crop yields and quality by optimizing their fertilization practices by comprehending nutrient surpluses or deficits. Soil testing also helps avoid fertilizer overuse, which can have negative effects on the environment and long-term economic viability.

FERTILIZATION AND SOIL AMENDMENTS

These two processes are essential to crop management and soil preparation. Farmers can improve the structure and fertility of their soil by adding the proper amendments once soil testing has identified any deficiencies or imbalances. Compost, manure, and cover crops are examples of organic resources that improve the texture, water retention, and microbial activity of soil to promote soil health.

Contrarily, fertilization entails the addition of nutrients through the use of organic or synthetic fertilizers. The nutrients needed by the crop and the makeup of the soil influence the fertilizer selection.

To guarantee that crops receive the essential nutrients at various phases of growth, timing and application rates must be carefully considered.

To reduce their negative effects on the environment, organic fertilizers, and precise application methods are prioritized in sustainable farming practices.

IRRIGATION TECHNIQUES

In regions where natural rainfall is insufficient for ideal plant growth, irrigation is a crucial component of crop management. Effective irrigation techniques are necessary to guarantee water availability for the duration of the growing season.

Several variables, including crop type, soil type, and water availability, influence the choice of irrigation techniques, including flood irrigation, sprinkler systems, and drip irrigation.

Farmers can apply the appropriate amount of water at the appropriate time thanks to precision irrigation, which is made possible by technological advancements like weather forecasts and soil moisture monitors. This avoids problems like soil erosion and waterlogging while also conserving water supplies.

Using sustainable irrigation techniques enhances agricultural cultivation's overall success and water efficiency.

PEST AND DISEASE MANAGEMENT

Careful consideration is necessary for these crucial crop management components. To reduce the impact of pests and diseases, integrated pest management, or IPM, is a comprehensive strategy that includes chemical, cultural, and biological control techniques.

To stop pest and disease problems from getting worse, it is crucial to monitor and discover problems early.

Crop rotation and companion planting are two examples of cultural practices that are important in managing pests and diseases. Farmers can interrupt insect life cycles and establish a more balanced environment by carefully arranging their crops in the field. Furthermore, when needed, the prudent application of pesticides aids in outbreak containment without endangering the sustainability of the ecosystem.

Crop rotation and companion planting are two age-old agricultural techniques that support sustainable crop management, insect control, and healthy soil. Planting various crops in the same field one after the other over a certain amount of time is known as crop rotation. T

his method cnhances soil structure, breaks down disease and pest cycles, and maximizes nutrient uptake.

To optimize benefits to both parties, companion planting entails carefully positioning compatible crops close to one another. Certain plants produce natural substances that serve as a natural pest deterrent or attract beneficial insects. Certain crop combinations also improve plant health overall and nutrient uptake.

A comprehensive strategy that includes soil testing, careful application of fertilizers and amendments, effective irrigation techniques, integrated pest and disease management, and the use of crop rotation and companion planting is necessary for successful soil preparation and crop management. The long-term sustainability of agriculture is ensured while yields are optimized and the health of the soil ecosystem is preserved by implementing ecologically friendly and sustainable practices.

CHAPTER FIVE

HOW TO PLANT AND GROW PUMPKINS

SELECTION AND GERMINATION OF SEEDS

The crucial stage of choosing and germination of seeds is where the cultivation of pumpkins starts. Selecting premium pumpkin seeds is essential since it has a direct impact on how well the entire growing process goes. Growers and farmers should choose seeds from reliable suppliers, making sure the seeds are clean, fresh, and the right kind for their particular growing environment.

To increase the likelihood of a healthy pumpkin crop, it is advisable to test for germination before planting to determine the viability of the seeds.

 The first stage of germination is when pumpkin seeds begin to sprout and grow into seedlings. The best soil for seed germination is one that drains well and is rich in nutrients.

For pumpkin germination, the optimal soil temperature falls between 60°F and 95°F (15°C and 35°C). It is imperative to maintain sufficient moisture during this phase, and it is advised to regularly check the soil's moisture content to avoid drying out or flooding, two conditions that might impede germination.

DIRECT SEEDING AND TRANSPLANTING

 In pumpkin production, two popular techniques— transplanting and direct seeding—each have a unique set of benefits and drawbacks. Pumpkin seedlings are transplanted onto their ultimate growing location after being started inside or in a controlled setting. By starting the growth season early, this technique enables a longer growing season and possibly larger yields. Seedlings must be handled carefully during transplanting to prevent breaking their fragile roots.

On the other hand, direct seeding entails sowing pumpkin seeds straight into the soil that has been ready for them to grow to maturity.

This is a less complicated strategy that does not require transplanting, but it can be more vulnerable to environmental stresses like bad weather or pest damage. For both direct seeding and transplanting, timing is critical, taking into account the local environment and dates of frost.

SUITABLE PLANTING AND SPACING METHODS

To maximize the potential of a pumpkin crop, it is essential to achieve the optimum spacing and use suitable planting procedures. Depending on the particular variety being grown, the ideal distance between pumpkin plants varies, but as a general rule of thumb, allows 3 to 5 feet (1 to 1.5 meters) between plants. This distance reduces competition for sunshine and nutrients while allowing the sprawling vines enough room to develop.

Making hills or mounds for the pumpkin seeds is part of the planting process. To improve germination and encourage early development, mounds improve soil drainage and help warm the soil. It is best to thin the seedlings later after sowing several seeds in a mound to ensure ideal spacing and avoid overcrowding. Mulching the area surrounding the base of the plants aids in temperature regulation, weed suppression, and soil moisture retention.

MAINTENANCE AND CARE OF PUMPKIN PLANTS

A good yield depends on regular care and upkeep after the pumpkins are established. To maintain constant soil moisture, regular irrigation is crucial, particularly during dry spells. On the other hand, it is equally crucial to refrain from overwatering, as this may result in root rot and other problems.

Adding a layer of organic mulch to the soil helps control temperature, weed growth, and moisture retention.

Another important part of caring for pumpkin plants is fertilization. A balanced fertilizer that is high in nutrients like potassium, phosphorus, and nitrogen is beneficial for the healthy growth of vines and fruits. Adherence to the required rates and timing of fertilization is crucial to prevent over fertilization, which may lead to excessive growth of foliage at the cost of fruit yield.

Managing diseases and pests is essential to growing pumpkins. It's crucial to regularly check for pests like aphids, squash bugs, and cucumber beetles. When necessary, appropriate control techniques like using certified pesticides or natural predators should be put into place. Prevention is key to combating diseases like bacterial wilt and powdery mildew. Some preventive strategies include using disease-resistant pumpkin types, adequate air circulation, and appropriate spacing.

Growing pumpkins successfully requires a well-thought-out strategy that starts with careful seed selection and germination and continues with transplanting or direct seeding, appropriate spacing, planting methods, and meticulous plant upkeep.

CHAPTER SIX

HARVESTING AND HANDLING AFTER HARVEST

CALCULATING THE EASE OF HARVEST

A crucial component of agriculture is figuring out when to harvest crops to maximize their quality and maturity. Many variables, including the type of crop, the surrounding environment, and the intended use, affect harvest readiness. When deciding when to harvest, farmers usually use a combination of physiological signs, visual clues, and experience.

Color, size, texture, hardness, and other characteristics are important in detecting when fruits and vegetables like pumpkins arc ready. Furthermore, particular markers are frequently taken into account, such as variations in the color of the stem or how simple it is to extract a fruit from the plant. To maximize output and quality, harvest readiness must be determined precisely.

METHODS OF HARVESTING

The type of crop, its physical attributes, and the target market all influence the harvesting process selection. Harvesting can be done manually, mechanically, or by combining the two methods. Because pumpkins are a delicate fruit, harvesting them by hand is a typical procedure.

To minimize damage, the fruit is gently cut from the vine using hand tools like shears or knives. On the other hand, large-scale enterprises with crops that have a more resilient structure might use mechanical harvesters. The choice of the right harvesting method is essential for maintaining the crop's integrity during the process as well as for efficiency.

HOW TO CURE AND STORE PUMPKINS

Pumpkins go through a curing procedure to improve their flavor, texture, and general quality after harvest. Curing entails letting the pumpkins air dry for a predetermined amount of time in a warm, well-ventilated place. This procedure extends the skin's shelf life, lowers its moisture content, and toughens the skin. To stop rotting and increase shelf life, cured pumpkins are kept in a dry, cool place. To keep the pumpkins fresh and stop disease growth, proper storage conditions are necessary. Growers can utilize a range of storage techniques, like stacking or utilizing specialized containers, to maximize available space and maintain the quality of the harvested pumpkins for a longer duration.

SORTING AND QUALITY CONTROL

A critical phase in the post-harvest handling process is quality control, which guarantees that only goods that satisfy predetermined criteria are sold. Harvested pumpkins are carefully inspected and sorted according to several factors, including size, color, and general quality. Quality control procedures aid in identifying and separating pumpkins that are infected or damaged from those that are fit for sale.

Sophisticated technologies are being used more often to improve the accuracy and efficiency of the sorting process, such as automated sorting systems and quality checking equipment. This methodical approach not only satisfies customer demands but also enhances the agricultural enterprise's overall success and market reputation.

CHAPTER SEVEN

PROMOTING AND BUYING PUMPKINS

FINDING YOUR IDEAL CUSTOMER BASE

Determining your target market is essential for developing an effective marketing and sales plan in the pumpkin industry. You can better target your products and promotional activities to the unique needs and preferences of your target audience by getting to know who they are as potential consumers.

Your target audience may consist of local businesses in need of big pumpkin purchases for events, families searching for seasonal decorations, or even people interested in carving pumpkins.

You can identify the traits and inclinations of your ideal clientele by carrying out surveys, market research, and demographic data analysis.

CREATING A LOGO FOR YOUR PUMPKIN COMPANY

Building a solid brand is crucial to being noticed in the crowded pumpkin industry. Customers should be positively impacted by your brand and be able to identify with the distinctive features of your pumpkins. Take into account elements like the caliber of your pumpkins, the techniques you use in your farming, and any unique characteristics that set your goods apart from competitors. Develop a distinctive and reliable brand for your pumpkin business with a memorable logo, unified packaging, and an engaging brand narrative.

MARKETING PLANS FOR SALES OF PUMPKINS

Using successful marketing techniques is essential to growing your pumpkin business and increasing revenue. You may increase your reach by utilizing both digital and conventional marketing channels. Make use of social media channels to share interesting content, engage with your audience, and display eye-catching photos of your pumpkins. To generate excitement about your company, you may also think about working with regional influencers, holding pumpkin-themed events, or running discounts. Because the pumpkin market is seasonal and community-focused, word-of-mouth marketing can have a particularly big impact.

REGIONAL MARKETS

Selling pumpkins at local markets is a tried-and-true, yet effective method. By putting up booths at farmers' markets, fall fairs, and other neighborhood gatherings, you can establish direct contact with local clients. Provide freebies, strike up discussions, and create an unforgettable experience to cultivate a following of devoted clients.

Another way to expand distribution is to collaborate with nearby companies like florists or grocery stores. Success in local markets requires you to design your product line and marketing strategy around the preferences of the local population.

INTERNET-BASED SALES

Adding internet sales to your pumpkin marketing plan will greatly increase the size of your clientele. Make an interesting and easy-to-use website where clients can peruse your assortment of pumpkins, discover more about your company, and easily place orders. By putting in place an e-commerce infrastructure, you may expand your consumer base beyond your neighborhood and even pursue national or even worldwide sales. Make sure your online presence is search engine optimized, and use social media to increase website traffic.

STRATEGIES FOR PRICING AND PACKAGING

It's critical to carefully consider your pumpkins' pricing and packaging to draw in customers and maintain profitability. When determining prices, take into account perceived value, market demand, and production costs. You may serve a wider spectrum of clients by providing multiple sizes and kinds at different pricing points. In addition to protecting the pumpkins, packaging should visually represent your company. Vibrant and environmentally friendly packaging can raise the perceived value of your goods, influencing consumers' decisions to buy and promoting brand loyalty. To remain competitive in the pumpkin sector, examine and modify your pricing and packaging tactics regularly depending on consumer feedback and market developments.